FALLING IN THE DIRECTION OF UP

KURT LUCHS

Sagging
Meniscus

Printed in the United States of America.
Set in Mrs Eaves XLwith LaTeX.

ISBN: 978-1-952386-07-7 (paperback)
Library of Congress Control Number: 2020950717

Sagging Meniscus Press
Montclair, New Jersey
saggingmeniscus.com

To my brothers and sisters
and to Sheryl

"*Grief is subversive, undermining the quiet agreement to behave and be in control of our emotions. It is an act of protest that declares our refusal to live numb and small. There is something feral about grief, something essentially outside the ordained and sanctioned behaviors of our culture. Because of that, grief is necessary to the vitality of the soul. Contrary to our fears, grief is suffused with life-force.... It is not a state of deadness or emotional flatness. Grief is alive, wild, untamed and cannot be domesticated. It resists the demands to remain passive and still. We move in jangled, unsettled, and riotous ways when grief takes hold of us. It is truly an emotion that rises from the soul.*"

—Francis Weller, *The Wild Edge of Sorrow*

Contents

III. The Sound of Water

IV. Falling in the Direction of Up

FALLING IN THE DIRECTION OF UP

I.

Feral Grief

The House of Memory

Last night once again I walked
in the house of my youth,
not quite our family home
as we were never really a family
and it was never really home.
In later years we had it painted
an arsenic green, but when I return
to it now it is always
the filthy white I knew from the first.
When it comes into view
I begin to weep. The people within
were torn down long before the house was.
Yet some of them are still standing
after a fashion, and so too
miraculously, horribly,
is the house of pain,
the house of memory.
To remember is to suffer.
To forget would be to lose yourself
and everything that made you.
Caught between these two imponderables
I tread the vanished floor and run
my fingers over the cryptic
graffiti on the ghostly walls:
"Ours is not to reason why,
ours is but to flip and fly," and
"No smoking even if you're on fire."
Soon the only people who know
what these words mean will be gone,
and where the house of memory
will be then, no one can say.
Meanwhile I walk in it,
marveling, shuddering,
knowing I have left it
but it will never leave me.

Suzie

The only true democrat in our household,
you would bite anyone
who passed too close to the couch,
darting from behind or beneath it
like a streak of auburn vengeance,
snapping at trousers, dresses, ankles,
leaving marks, breaking skin,
or most satisfying of all, drawing blood
before retreating to plot the next assault.
We lived in fear. I think you lived
for the scent of that fear,
more stimulating than the smell of fresh meat,
though with any luck you'd get a taste of meat also.
If two children were fighting
you always picked the winning side,
adding your teeth marks
to the loser's humiliation.
Whenever our father beat us
you would take his side too,
which is how some of your bites
flowered red among purple bruises.
Your mother was a Schnauzer,
your father a Dachshund
(how on earth did he manage it?),
making you a canine blitzkrieg,
a stormtrooper in fur.
Later, gray and white crept up
your orange-brown hair,
your mad eyes filled with cataracts,
you slowed down enough that sometimes
we could escape your jaws.
After you died, we cremated most of you
but kept your pale yellow skull to bake
in the crook of a tree,
a warning to trespassers,
an inspiration to the vicious and cruel.

The Blizzard of 1967 (Chicago)

The snow was already falling when we awoke
that Thursday morning, January 26th.
The weatherman (they were almost all
men back then) predicted only four inches
so we dressed and walked to school as usual.
Then the flakes became clumps
like the frosted fossils of arctic milkweed pods
and they just kept coming all day,
past the twilight as we staggered home
sinking with every step, and into the deepening night.
There was no school Friday when the snow
finally stopped around 10 a.m., having reached
23 inches, a record that has held ever since.
The blizzard that was an infuriating frustration
for adults was pure delight to the rest of us.
We spent much of that weekend sledding
where we could never sled before
and jumping off of roofs into snowbanks
that were taller than many of us.
There were tragedies, too, of course—
a rash of lootings in the city,
a little girl gunned down in the crossfire
between looters and police, several people
who suffered heart attacks shoveling snow
and even a minister run over by a snow plow,
poor devil, poor snow angel.
What I recall most clearly though
is the gentle hiss of the snow falling
like an air mattress springing a tiny leak
or the world folding in on itself in slow motion:
the illusory sound of peace in which,
for once, I could sleep through the night.

Father's Belt

I don't like holding his pants up.
He's gone to fat since his discharge
from the Marines, and frankly
it's a chore. Nor do I care
for being hung in the closet,
left in the dark between two dress shirts
that haven't a clue
as to the horrors and pleasures that life holds.
The worst thing that ever happened to them
was a ketchup stain on the cuff,
easily removed by the most inept of dry cleaners,
his dry cleaner. No, what I like
is when he takes me off, and not to put away.
I like when his rage comes bubbling up,
never far from the surface,
set off by whatever you little bastards
have done today, it doesn't really matter what,
does it? Then his hands are strong again,
I feel his love through me
as he folds me in half and makes me
snap against myself with a loud crack.
That's to make you afraid.
It hardly seems necessary
yet I assure you, it's an essential part
of the ceremony, it's foreplay.
The smell of fear is an aphrodisiac.
Then all at once I'm whistling
through the air, my flesh meets yours
in a mad rush, and there is joy in heaven,
my ecstasy cannot be contained.
The red welts come quickly, purple bruises
will follow, and sometimes if his passion
is fierce enough there's a bit of blood
from my buckle end, the sweetest release.
He says he loves you, he does it all for love.
I don't mind. I know it's me he really loves.
I love him too.
And I love you, all seven of you,
each receiving my affections differently
because love is unending, there's always more.
Do you realize, aside from him
you're the only ones I ever get to touch?

Abduction

Brad, he said his name was, the man
about 30 in a red Mustang
who offered me a ride
that summer day between 7th and 8th grade,
the Summer of Love.
Every other radio was blaring *Sgt. Pepper*
but Brad was tuned to the classical station.
Debussy. Satie.
He was an adult in a suit.
I said yes.
All too soon he turned the wrong way
and then again and again, fast enough
that I couldn't think of jumping out.
We stopped miles out of town
on a dirt road in a cornfield.
He couldn't look at me.
Sweat glistened on his forehead
as he spoke of what he wanted to do.
His right hand was moist too,
crawling into my lap
like a fleshy pink tarantula.
I backed against the door on the passenger side.
I told him I only liked girls.
He said that was all right, he'd pay me.
Then he started to cry,
sobbing on my shoulder, his fingers
suddenly grasping with a different need,
the need not to be hated for his need.
I realized the power had shifted in my favor.
I patted him on the back, told him
it was all right and said it was time
to go home now.
He never said another word.
I never told a soul.
What amazes me most
is that I can still enjoy Satie.
Debussy was permanently ruined.
To this day the opening notes of *La Mer*
make me weep, I'm not sure for whom.

The Mystery of Evil

You surprised no one by dying of an overdose.
Was it glue or oven cleaner?
I can no longer recall, but I know
you enjoyed them both to the full.
Your time on earth was brief, though not brief enough
to keep you from torturing a cat to death
with leftover fireworks and a refrigerator box.
Why is sharing the pain always easier than sharing the joy?
Or perhaps you had no joy to share
other than the joy of glue and oven cleaner and torture.
At a certain point all arguments become circular.
The best thing about you was your gay uncle
who would recite Tennessee Williams
to a roomful of teenagers who thought he was making it up.
He referred to the home where he grew up as a living hell,
and I'm sure it was no different for you,
yet somehow you didn't emerge from it
tenderly quoting Tennessee Williams, and he did.
All these years later I still ponder it,
the mystery of evil, as I light the memory
of a roman candle and toss it in with you
in the refrigerator box of my mind.

To Michael Beasley, Who Beat My Turtles to Death

Why my mother kept letting you in the house
I'll never know.
It would always be when I was not at home.
Then she would resume her routine—
staring out the window while stirring
a cup of tea that was at least half sugar,
all that sweetness wasted on a zombie
of post-partum depression,
seven feral children in ten years.
You, of course, did not dawdle.
You got right down to business, heading straight
to the room I shared with my three brothers
and removing my pet turtles from the terrarium
where they must have thought they were safe.
The last thing they would see was
our peeling ceiling and whatever
blunt object your grubby little fist wielded.
One time it was my prized possession
a Talking G.I. Joe figurine capable of uttering
half a dozen urgent battlefield phrases.
After that his neck bent at an odd angle,
and whenever I pulled his string
all he could say was, "Medic!
Get that stretcher up here!"
But there was no medic for my turtles
or for me.

A Typical Weekend in My Young Life

After realizing that nonstop infidelity and arguments
lifted from *Who's Afraid of Virginia Woolf*
were not leading to a happy marriage,
our parents embarked on a therapy weekend
somewhere on Chicago's north shore that Summer of Love.
They left their seven offspring to the tender mercies
of one Jack Devlin, recently fired from our father's place of work
for abusing both alcohol and cocaine,
currently unemployed and enjoying a week-long binge
but otherwise a model citizen and ideal caregiver.
Upon entering our home, eyes wide and bloodshot,
wiry black hair standing on end, ruddy face dripping with sweat,
he marched straight to the record player, rifled through a stack
of 45's, selected one and began miming with ferocious concentration
to the Rolling Stones singing, "Play with Fire."
We giggled nervously at first, but the novelty began to pall
after half an hour of repeats, interrupted only by him pausing
to sniff some powder from a vial and take a pull from a flask.
Jack noticed one of our half-dozen cats, the lovely Morna,
and proceeded to forcibly share some of his powder with her.
She yowled, raced outside, clawed her way up a poplar tree,
had some kind of seizure and fell, never to be quite right after that.
We gaped at Jack, uncertain what to do, not believing
what we had just witnessed. He turned his attention to our
three-year-old sister, preparing to give some powder to her.
His eyes grew wider as he said that he wanted
to write his name on her bellybutton with his tongue.
My older sister and I snapped out of our trance,
gathered up our siblings and walked quickly to Northside Park
half a mile away, where there was a pay phone.
We called our parents and waited. Our brothers and sisters
sobbed and wailed, worried about the fate of our other animals.
An hour later we returned home in time to see
our parents pulling into the driveway in our Citroen 2CV.
They were followed by a white van from a mental institution.
Two muscular men in white uniforms got out of the van
and entered our home. Five minutes later they emerged
with Jack Devlin kicking and screaming in between them,
wrapped in the loving arms of a straitjacket. They strapped him
into the back of the van and left. We never saw him again.
Aside from the cat, no one was physically injured or killed.
It was an unremarkable weekend much like all the others,
that sunny therapy weekend in the Summer of Love.

Rudy

Why would a man who hates dogs decide to run a kennel?
We grew up next to your canine death camp,
never knowing the answer, watching you withhold food and water
from the animals entrusted to your carelessness,
thinking that endless yips, barks, howls and growls
were normal for these tormented creatures.
We learned to hate dogs almost as much as you did.
We saw them cower from the ever-present garden hose
you carried, more to punish than to clean, and we realized
why they were so docile and grateful
when their unsuspecting owners finally returned for them.
If your prisoners could have turned from their own troubles
to our house, they might've thought they were looking
into a mirror. Why would two people who hate each other
and children decide to have seven of them?
We never deciphered that riddle either.
Oh, we were fed and clothed and warehoused after a fashion,
but deprived of love and light like unwanted plants
left to die in the basement.
Some of us did live down there, blind cave salamanders
inventing games to pass the time, including one
we named after you. We called it "Doing the Rudy."
We would don a faded Hawaiian shirt,
step into an arthritic shuffle with our arms swinging slowly,
let a candy cigarette dangle from our lower lip
like one of your Pall Malls, and start humming
"Thanks for the Memories" in the key of senile dementia.
And so the time did pass. Sometimes, in the night hours
alone in my apartment, I still hear distant howls,
and some buried part of me longs
to do the Rudy, to shuffle past each rusting cage,
to undo every lock and let the suffering find release at last.

Dean Natkin

If ever there was such a thing as a gentleman drug dealer,
a pusher of taste and refinement, it was you.
You came with the rest of our parents' Chicago Mensa friends
and you were always welcome in every discussion
so your intelligence was not in doubt.
What's curious is that no one seemed to hold
your occupation against you, perhaps because we knew
you only peddled weed and hallucinogens, not the hard stuff.
Nor would you sell anything stronger than grass
to children, as I learned when I tried to score some LSD from you.
You advised me that mescaline was gentler and more reliable,
and that any person with my brains and initiative
should be able to synthesize that for themselves.
I never knew whether you were straight, gay or bisexual,
never saw you arrive with your arm around anybody,
though unlike some of our parents' circle
I'm pretty sure you were no pedophile
as you didn't make a pass at me or my siblings.
What you loved fiercely and beyond all reason
was jazz, the melodic sweetness of Guaraldi
or the angular angst of Coltrane, it didn't matter,
you enjoyed snapping your fingers and doffing
your Maynard G. Krebs beret in the presence of the masters.
You understood we were musically deprived
and that the best way to reach us was with rock—
Beatles, Dylan, Airplane, Donovan, Cream.
Once I caught you listening without irony to Peter, Paul and Mary.
Then came a memorable July Saturday when you brought over
the first two Firesign Theatre albums of surreal, multilayered comedy,
Waiting for the Electrician or Someone Like Him
and *How Can You Be in Two Places at Once*
When You're Not Anywhere at All.
I was 15 and had finally scored some acid
from a fellow student better at chemistry than I was.
Those records took the top of my head off
and it hasn't come back down yet. Thus was I led
down dark doorways into my own subconscious
and I began to write, and today I write of you, Dean Natkin,
your compassion for feral children, your pure friendship,
your very pure dope and the precious gift
of laughing together at our nearly human madness.

Christmas Nineteen-Sixty-Something

By that time we were hanging the tree from a hook
in the living room ceiling, to keep our six or seven cats
from climbing into it, batting ornaments off and toppling it over.
All in vain, because they simply started leaping into it
from the couch, turning it into a holiday pendulum
that shed ornaments even faster and from higher up and
sometimes brought the whole thing down with a tinkling crash.
While other families were gathered around the tree
singing carols, our father played his favorite records
again and again—*Hitler's Inferno, Volumes 1 and 2*—
and had us goosestep through the house to the rousing strains
of "The Horst Wessel Song" and other Nazi anthems.
(He was not a Nazi, merely an American advertising man,
a gifted copywriter with a sick sense of humor
and a soul-deep appreciation of effective propaganda.)
It would be years before we would see anything odd about this.
One year, though, he became conventional for a few terrifying
moments, and tried to mimic what our neighbors were doing.
He lined all seven of us up under the hanging tree,
put mimeographed sheets of Christmas songs into our hands
and demanded in his best Marine Corps drill sergeant manner
that we start celebrating the birth of the baby Jesus
with enthusiasm, real or counterfeit, it didn't matter.
We were a sorry lot of carolers, our faint, trembling voices
dying in the lower branches of the tree. He was not impressed.
"Sing, damn you, sing!" he screamed at the top of his lungs
over and over and over and over and over and over.
Merry Christmas! Sieg heil! God bless us everyone.

Burn Marks

As dusk descended we built a bonfire,
the flames blending with the last of the sunset,
the smoke merging with the new night.
We pretended we were natives of some faraway place,
dancing around the fire and chanting nonsense guttural syllables.
One of us, I don't recall which, plucked a burning branch
from the blaze and waved it in the air,
writing on the dark like neon.
Then each of us did it. Then we started playing tag
with the glowing embers at the ends of the sticks
and the game got serious, shirts and blue jeans singed, ruined,
the unmistakable stench of melting hair
and the high-pitched screams of those branded on naked flesh.
Our parents did not intervene, absorbed in their own savage game.
I burned someone and was burnt in turn down my left forearm.
The wound healed quickly. The massive scar lasted decades,
fading slowly and disappearing completely
in the last year or so, I didn't notice exactly when.
Now there is only a spark of memory, the least reliable witness,
to testify to the skin-deep nature of civilization.

Tokyo Rose

I.

That name was never yours,
though bestowed after the fact
by your adoring audience: Allied troops
in the South Pacific.
Nor was the name even exclusive to you.
Every woman broadcasting Japanese propaganda
got called the same thing,
and there were many of you, working in shifts
around the clock to discourage our boys in uniform.
In this task you were notably unsuccessful
with your dance music program "The Zero Hour"
(after the Mitsubishi A6M Zero fighter plane).
Later surveys revealed that only ten percent of your listeners
felt demoralized. Eighty-four percent
considered your show good entertainment
and quite a few thought you were really on their side.
How difficult it is for lonely men to resist
a woman with a lovely voice.
Maybe it was something in your voice
that told them you were lonely too.
If they only knew!
You were an American just like them,
visiting a sick aunt in Japan
when Pearl Harbor was attacked.
Unable to return once war was declared,
unable to stay with family in Japan
as an American citizen,
cut off from any aid or comfort from your parents
back in the USA because they were soon
imprisoned in an Arizona internment camp
by the most popular president of all time,
what were your choices?
The ugly truth is that your beautiful voice
was all you had to trade for bread.
So you spent the war behind a microphone,
cooing to men in submarines and destroyers,
aircraft carriers and troop transports,
while the latest big band hits played
like the undertow of a long, long wave.

II.

After the war, with nuclear fallout still fresh
in the ashen craters once known as Hiroshima and Nagasaki,
your real name became infamous
when you tried to reenter your homeland.
The American authorities announced that you,
Iva Toguri D'Aquino,
were the one and only true Tokyo Rose.
They arrested you, tried you and convicted you
of treason, only the seventh person
in our history to receive that dishonor.
You served six years in prison
before being released in 1956.
Two decades later you earned a full pardon
from President Ford when certain facts came to light:
you had refused to renounce your US citizenship
despite intense pressure from the Japanese government,
which declared you an enemy alien
and denied you a war ration card.
You lived on seven dollars a month,
yet managed to set enough aside
to smuggle food to friends in POW camps.
Your radio programs were subtly subversive,
apolitical and fun. Listeners could hear
the finger quotes around the lame propaganda.
Then the two main witnesses against you
recanted their testimony and admitted
they had been coerced.
Some things never change.

III.

My siblings and I knew you
as the proprietor of J. Toguri Mercantile,
a seller of Asian goods and novelties
near the corner of Clark and Belmont in Chicago.
At first we were fascinated by the exotic candies
and the paper pellets that would bloom
into every kind of flower when dropped in a glass of water.
You showed us these things without ever saying
more than "hello," "goodbye," "thank you"
and "good day."
Known so long only for your voice
you now chose to have none.
Soon my attention turned to the landscapes on your walls.
I developed a passion for Japanese brush painting
and determined to learn it, talent be damned.

I began a course at the Art Institute,
fell in love with my Japanese teacher
(I think she loved me a little too)
and bought all of my art supplies from you.
When I showed you my feeble paintings
you would only nod and smile.
Who knows what you really thought?
You kept your own counsel to the end,
refusing to be drawn on questions about the war.
Thanks to my father I knew better than to ask.
You let me draw you though,
with my childish brush strokes
that could no more capture you
than a federal subpoena or an off-camera cameo
in *Destination Tokyo* alongside Cary Grant.
I don't know what happened to that painting.
Like you, it has disappeared from history.
I wish I could look on your kind, quiet, closed face
one more time, dear Tokyo Rose.

Edgar Allan Crow

A farmer's wife in West Chicago found you
starving, wings broken, barely alive,
a baby crow without a future,
and brought you into the barn to try
to nurse you back to something resembling health.
As you ate and gained strength day by day
your marvelous gift for mimicry emerged.
Your tiny crow voice learned to imitate
cows, chickens, pigs, goats, sheep, cats and dogs
with hilarious accuracy, eventually causing
no end of confusion for the farmer and his wife.
And that's how you came to us, still broken
but now with a vaudeville act to earn your keep.
Though we had no farm, we did have
chickens and geese and cats and dogs in abundance.
We named you after the poet
and taught you to say "Nevermore."
The Willowbrook Wildlife Sanctuary
clipped and set your wings, which kept you
flightless until you were tame and acclimated to a cage.
You adorably called them "Brookwillow,"
getting the syllables right but the order wrong.
We understood: English was not your first language.
You deeply resented sharing your cage
with the chickens, considering them little more
than vegetables with beaks.
You would throw the rooster's morning cry
back at him with an audible sneer.
When you could finally fly, sometimes you'd swoop
down and peck him on his idiot head.
We'd reach through the wire to pet you
until you purred like a cat,
blinking slowly with your sky-blue inner eyelids.
After our baby sister was born
you added the wail of a miniature human
to your repertoire of voices.
"Somebody check the baby!" our mother would yell.
"It's Edgar," we sighed in reply.
You learned to imitate her as well,
fooling us many times with your rendition
of her favorite phrase, "Shut the door!"
"It *is* shut!" we screamed.
She would sigh, "That was Edgar."
You appeared to prefer captivity.
If we left the cage door open

you never once ventured outside.
It seemed an idyllic life.
And then, as it usually does, love spoiled everything.
A lady crow we named Claw came to roost
in the maple tree overlooking your cage.
Her wiles were many. She used them all,
turning you against us.
One day we left the cage door open
and you flew up to her branch
and suddenly it was all over.
From that moment forward you took us
for enemies, the two of you following
us wherever we went, hurling abuse
upon us as you flew from tree to tree, as if to say,
"These are the ones! The torturers,
the cagers of crows, the brutalizers of birds!
Do not let them forget their crimes!"
We were happy for you, honestly we were,
but now we were the broken ones.
This went on for years, perhaps a decade.
At some point we realized that one of you
had died, the duet of diatribes
had become a single voice again,
though you'd grown so close to each other
we couldn't tell which one had perished
and which was still alive with solitary fury.
That hurt more than anything.
Then it was, our wayward echoer Edgar,
that we too learned to say, "Nevermore."

Boodina

She tried to teach me to hunt, the gray tabby
who appeared on our doorstep one day and never left.
Confident and self-contained, the essence of cathood,
she took pity on this child wandering the asylum grounds,
never sure where he stood with the other inmates
and always waiting for the next blow to fall.
She seemed made for our household, being impervious
to random screams and bellows of Marine Corps profanity.
Her response to all threats of domestic violence
was to silently dissolve into the vacant fields around us
and set to work tracking as if there was a bounty
on every stray rodent in town.
Her patience was boundless, though I was useless
in summer and not much better in winter.
At least after a snowfall I could see their tiny footprints
with the occasional swish of a tail between, like a signature
by Degas, and sometimes I would even spot a glimpse
of them disappearing into their hidey holes,
but I never came close to capturing one.
Boodina did, coolly, cleanly, without any visible excitement,
like a ping pong master holding a book in one hand
and a paddle in the other, not glancing up
as she batted them back and forth while stifling a yawn.
That was how I learned to catch mice at age six or seven,
and also that I never would catch any,
and that catching them was not the point.
The hunt was the thing, sniffing scents on the wind,
the glint of the cold winter sun, the crunch of snow,
the feel of dead brown grass in the hand and underfoot,
and every now and then, the sign of our elusive prey
leading us ever forward into fresh mysteries together.

The First Time

Much as our ancestors must've done it,
for us it happened in a field of long grass
in early autumn, before the first chill.
You felt a twinge of pain at the start
and winced without making a sound,
but then it was good for both of us.
It was all over quickly.
What does a boy of fifteen know about controlling desire?
As much as a man of six decades
knows about controlling the memories that wash over him,
surging forward, receding, surging forward, receding,
like the rhythm of your breath that day
in the late afternoon with clouds for a ceiling
and the earth for a bed.
Everything has changed. Nothing has changed!
The pebbles pushed forward by the surf of years
have neither worn down nor sunk back into the sea.
These aquatic metaphors are more than mere fancy.
Not so long ago the whole Midwest was an ocean.
If you dug down a few meters below where we lay
you would find fossil fish imprinted on the stone,
for the earth also has its memories
that persist, and perhaps in the endless eating
of its own crust, it too turns them over and over,
thinking back on the beginnings of things.

Northside Park

Sun. Sky. Clouds. Shafts of light, then shade.
Wild grass. Cottonwood trees. Mornings that drift into afternoons.
Afternoons that drift into eternity.
The green lagoon overflowing its banks, or not.
Painted turtles sunning themselves on logs or stones.
Snapping turtles poking their rough-hewn heads out of the muck.
Frogs. Toads. Every once in a while, a salamander blinking in the rain.
A home away from the home that is not a home.
A world within the world, now only
a world within the world within.
Happy hours that become days.
Days that become years.
Years not worth remembering except for sun, sky, clouds.
That's all. And that's enough.

II.

Night and Morning

Night in the City

Feel the radio
dancing in a corner,
insect music on my forehead.
Fog sustains the city.
Cars die by the thousands,
pale headlights turning from moons
to stars, then blinking
out of sight.
No one knows
how many people are lost tonight,
or sleeping.

3:07 a.m.

Silence so deep you can hear
that moth combing its antennae.
The trees are asleep on their feet, oblivious.
A single leaf yawns, turns over.
At the hint of a breeze the grass
pulls the bedclothes tighter.
I should mention how the moonlight
looks but I can barely keep my eyes open
so instead I'll say what it sounds like:
like a dining room in a
long-foreclosed mansion where the finest
china has just been laid out on
the finest tablecloth by the
ghost of the late butler
who nodded off while looking
for the spoons.
The secret joy of the hour
is that anything could happen
and nothing ever does.

Flying

None of us has wings, yet here we are,
higher than any bird and traveling
nearly as fast as the scream
of our own engines.
"Eight miles high" may sing better,
but it's really 6.6 miles,
still an impossible-to-believe miracle
that never quite palls, because it's true.
From here, at dusk, our human cities
pulse gently, luminescent jellyfish
spreading their tendrils into the dark
declivities between mountains.
Impossible to believe anything
too terrible could happen amid such glories.
Nonetheless, under every shimmering dot
lies a life full of secret grief, secret torment
that no earthly beauty can assuage,
and in each collection of dots
a murder here, a rape there,
a child struck for no reason.
Though my love for this world
remains unrequited
I will go on loving her
even as I move faster and farther away
over her unending curve.

To the Tenth Planet

What do you look like?
We may never know.
Now I understand the man
who walks into a bar
just after the most beautiful
woman walks out: she has
become invisible but he
can feel her absence tugging
at everyone who remains.
Their tiny perturbations
leave no doubt that
something wonderful has left us
and still has the power
to move us.
Your gravity does this,
causing the outer bodies
of our solar system
to shiver ever so slightly,
though no one has actually seen you.
I call you the tenth planet
because I've not quite
got over Pluto's pitiful demotion.
For me there can never
be another ninth.
Apparently you live
in the Kuiper Belt,
otherwise known as the Siberia
of our corner of the galaxy.
I'd welcome you warmly
to our little family of sun circlers,
except that would be
presumptuous and ignorant.
You've been here all along,
patiently waiting for your
beauty (yes, I'm sure now
it's beauty) to be discovered.

A Party

The other night I went to a party where most of the other attendees
were retired or headed there fast. They spoke contemptuously of their jobs
and longingly of the imagined life of ease. One man, a metallurgy teacher
at a technical college, was only months away from retirement. "I don't see
my students as students any longer," he said. "What do you mean?" I said.
"I mean I picture their empty heads as blocks of wood, and I see myself
putting them into a vise and twirling the handle until they snap," he said.
"You certainly are overdue for a long rest, Tom," I replied, moving on
while keeping one eye on him. I met a woman named Grace who was in
the business of trying to impart computer skills to senior citizens with
dementia. I said, "You have chosen a difficult but noble path." She looked
at me as if seeing me for the first time, which in fact she was. She leaned
closer, put one hand up to her mouth, and whispered, "Most days it's all
I can do not to smother them with a pillow." "Of course," I said,
backing away. "I understand completely." Another woman was sobbing
quietly in a dark corner and saying over and over again, "My name is
Abigail, my name is Abigail." I shook her gently and said, "I think
we've established that, Abigail. What else do you have to say for yourself?"
Her eyes would not meet mine. "I was an accountant," she said, "but what
I really loved was making pottery. I quit my job so I could spend more
time doing what I loved. I bought a kiln so big I could barely get it
into my basement. And now I don't do anyone's books, and I don't make pottery
either. I just sit watching the flames in the kiln, trying to think of a reason
not to crawl inside with them." When she finally looked up at me I realized
she must've spent some time in the kiln after all because she was nothing
but a skeleton dressed in charred and smoking rags. The eye sockets in her
skull were black and hollow. As my own eyes adjusted to the darkness
I saw that everyone at this party was a skeleton. Everyone but me.
I quickly grabbed my coat from the closet and made for the door.
The hostess stopped me and said, "Where are you going? The party's
just getting started." "Too much excitement for me," I said. "Besides,
I have to get up for work tomorrow."

"Outside it has stopped . . ."

Outside it has stopped snowing,
the pale glory that had turned every withered tree
into a throne for the king.
How quiet everything is,
as though he might still return.

Inside it goes on snowing,
the hiss swallowing up the last cries
of all the things that must die in a man
if the man is to go on living.
No wonder we feel immortal—
we have died so often!
The heart, strangled a thousand times
in its bloody nest,
shudders with disgust and longing
and goes on stuttering . . .

The sun stares over my shoulder
at my shadow making an abyss in the white,
and in my heart the snow goes on falling.

At the Dentist

It's almost a microcosm, a diorama
of life itself, the way the pain
is always so much worse than they tell you,
spitting blood and bits of enamel
mixed with antiseptic goo
until the idea of joy, or even happiness,
becomes simply an end to torture,
blessed and complete anesthesia.
The background music promises some kind of eternity,
watery guitar chords tumbling over each other
without ever reaching a resolution or forming a tune.
Ah, there it is! Life's meaningless, meandering
theme song, with the whine of the drill
the only counterpoint. I'm crying now, silently,
but my tears have no meaning either,
it's not as if my lover betrayed me again
or I had to endure a second childhood
despised by those who brought me into the world.
It's not as if my cat died.
The dark glasses they put on me hide everything.
"There, that didn't hurt, did it?" she chirps rhetorically.
I shake my head no, preferring not to lie with my mouth.
Most of the lies we tell are about our inability
to acknowledge pain. I'm no different
from the rest, I live in continual denial
of the agony within me and all around me.
And yet there is unspeakable joy too—
on the other side of the office window
a blue jay gobbles seeds from the feeder
meant to distract patients, his sheer delight
in being alive nearly as startling as his abrupt
upward departure, as if assumed into heaven
on an irresistible updraft,
the branches of the ash tree also reaching
toward the sky, which receives them both.
Suddenly I am elated, wistful and unbearably lonely
all at once, watching the bird and the branches
disappear into the blue, tasting the blood
on my tongue and hoping
the music of the mumbling guitar never stops.

My Dinner with Fahey

Once again I'm a real American, going nowhere
in particular but moving quickly from one empty,
well-lit building to the next, and going out of business
is my only business. Although you wouldn't
recognize my name I must be important—
when I considered buying a John Fahey CD
pictures of it followed me all over the internet
as if the whole future of our indigenous folk music
depended on me alone. Finally I relented
and gave them my credit card number,
musing that by the time Fahey was my age
he'd been dead for three years.
I recalled having dinner with him in a Chicago
Irish pub in the nineties, the lowest point of his life.
He drank beer after beer after beer
until when it came time for him to play,
he couldn't, and it wasn't only the alcohol
but diabetes, Epstein-Barr, a third divorce,
living in a welfare motel in Bend, Oregon,
and other ailments less obvious, perhaps a hell-hound
on his trail? The furious ghost of Charlie Patton?
Before he came undone that night we concocted a plan
to defy the restraining order from his third ex,
sneak into his own basement and retrieve
the master tapes for his two Reprise albums,
then still un-reissued. I would start a label
just for him, Lazarus Records, and if we couldn't
get legal permission we would become bootleggers.
Running afoul of the law clearly appealed to him
even more than getting his own music back out there.
It never happened. It turned out
I had a hell-hound on my own trail,
and Fahey amazed us all by cleaning up
later that decade and enjoying a comeback
that still hasn't stopped, even with his death
on the operating table amid a septuple bypass
decades ago. Every album has been properly reissued,
no credit to me or the unrisen Lazarus Records.
Thanks to our modern digital miracles
you can still get lost in the steep, sad canyons
between one note and another
on "Steam Boat Gwine Round De Bend."
Roll on, deep river, roll on.

The Sleep Test

I had a sleep test last night to determine whether I suffer
from sleep apnea. It started at 10 p.m.
At that hour they make you enter the hospital
through the Emergency Room, not the most
auspicious way to begin a routine procedure.
There was a man who had cut himself badly while
chopping vegetables and another
man who couldn't stop coughing.
He was a regular coughing machine, that guy.
When I reached the office on the third floor
a technician had me put on my pajamas
while he attached electrodes to various
parts of my body. As he got closer to my groin
I pondered whether to say something funny
like, "Not so free with the hands, there, Chester,"
but decided against it. For one thing, he probably wasn't
named Chester. For another, I didn't want to be
diagnosed with homophobia as well as sleep apnea.
When I was covered with wires and the equipment
was all set to record, I said, "I sure hope I pass.
I didn't study for the sleep test at all."
The technician said, "That's clever, considering
I've heard it eight million times." He dimmed
the lights and eventually I drifted off.
I think I dreamed throughout the night—vivid, colorful,
disturbing dreams, though when I awoke
I couldn't remember any details. I saw my
personal things on the end table where I had left them.
I looked in my wallet. The $300 was
still there, yet it appeared that one of the pictures of my
children was missing. Before I could wonder why
a doctor came in to remove the wires. "Well?" I said.
"Do I have sleep apnea?" "Too early to tell," he said.
"We'll have the results next week."
It was then that I noticed a large, transparent plastic
container on the counter. It was filled with an iridescent
liquid that pulsed and twirled and shifted
even as I watched, its long, tentacled shapes swiftly
merging into each other and reemerging in completely new
forms every few seconds. It seemed almost alive,
like a jellyfish in an aquarium.
"What's in there?" I said. "Dreams,"
said the doctor, and I knew he was telling
the truth. It made me feel dreamy just to look at it.
"My dreams?" I said. "Not anymore," he replied.

"Now just hold on a minute, pal," I said.
"You've been harvesting my dreams
without my permission?" "Harvesting isn't really
the word I would use," he said. "The word I would use
is stealing," I said. I was certain they must have
broken some law, but I had no way of knowing
which one, so I made one up. "You're in clear
violation of the Dream Copyright Act of 1997," I said,
trying to sound as officious as possible.
"There's no such thing, and you know it," the doctor sneered.
"According to the Dream Homesteading Act of 2003,
as soon as you go to sleep in this building
your dreams belong to us, and so do you. I could
take you to a bare room and lock you in there
until you mummified, and there's not a damn thing
you or your heirs or assigns could do about it, so watch it
with your fake legalese and get the hell out of here
or we'll send you straight back to dreamland."
I began to put my things in my pockets and prepared to leave,
but reluctantly. Dreamland sounded pretty good
right about then.

Notes from My Doppelganger

Kurt Luchs died quietly in his sleep last night.
Well, actually he was screaming plenty, but the pillow
I was holding over his face didn't let much of it out.
He made one last guttural noise, expired, and as a parting gift
soiled the bed. Why do people always fight the inevitable?
I shrugged and smiled. It was all the same to me.
I put on one of his suits, pitying his taste, and went to his job.
By noon I had promoted one person and fired two,
picking their names at random from a list of employees
I found in his desk. It doesn't matter much what one does, but one
should always do something, if merely to keep up appearances.
His girlfriend showed up expecting to go to lunch. I only
knew it was her because she walked right up and kissed me.
She seemed delighted at my suggestion to go to her place instead.
We made sweet love for an hour. Or rather, she made sweet love.
For me it was simply crazy good sex with a total stranger.
I got so caught up in the moment that I nearly offered her money.
The afternoon back at the office passed slowly as I pretended
to type at his work computer. I almost wished for a pillow to
scream into. When I got back to his apartment I expected
to find a smell and a corpse in the bed, but somehow
he was up and about again, puttering around in the kitchen.
Life is so persistent! Small wonder it has endured for so long
on this miserable excuse for a planet. He cleared his throat
and asked if I was still angry. I said no, it was all a misunderstanding.
"What do you want for dinner?" he said, somewhat hesitantly.
"I don't know," I said. "Why don't we order out?" As he turned
to pick up his phone, I hit him in the head three times
with a frying pan, sat on the couch and clicked the remote.

Night Inventory

We always have plenty of silence
but then there's so little demand.
Even when they think they want it
they often return it unopened,
and those weightless boxes take up a lot of space,
big and full of air.
We also have no shortage of crickets
though good luck trying to count them.
They seem to be everywhere
yet you can never actually find one.
Moonlight is still one of our biggest sellers—
whether from a full, half, sliver, or even a new moon—
it remains reliably popular
as other things go into and out of fashion.
Our shelves contain any number of strange new drinks
the thirst for which has not yet been invented,
and a variety of snacks which, sadly,
the stock clerk seems to have confused
with rat poison.
Management assumes no responsibility.
Time, of course, is short, a perennial problem.
No sooner do we get some in
than it flies out the door,
leaving no more trace
than our shadowy, anonymous customers.

The New Sangria

I had asked for a bottle of sangria, and that's what Roberta
appeared to have brought home, though it wasn't like any
bottle I'd ever seen before. There was
no brand name on the label for one thing.
In fact the label contained no printed matter
of any kind, simply a crude illustration
showing a silver-suited astronaut in space,
facing some sort of gigantic cosmic eye.
The eye was bleary and bloodshot, as if
it had already finished off the sangria.
I took a steak knife from a drawer in the counter
and began to peel the metal skin off of the cork,
defiantly returning the stare of that creepy
unblinking orb. At first it seemed to follow
me whichever way I turned my head. Then the red
veins started to throb and there was a sound
like somebody sucking on a straw
and a shimmering black cleft opened in mid-air
with a bluish-gray pseudopod tentatively
poking through it, feeling its way, exploring.
"Well, there's something you don't see every day,"
said Roberta. I almost sighed with relief.
"I'm glad you see it too," I said. "Of course
I see it too," she said. "We're drinking
the same wine, aren't we?" "We haven't
drunk any yet," I reminded her. Just then
the alien limb or whatever it was
touched her face, and as God is my
witness it began tickling her under the chin,
accompanied by a voice that gurgled,
"Cootchie-cootchie-coo!" Without thinking
I raised the steak knife high and slashed
that slimy thing in two. With an agonized shriek
the oozing stump withdrew through the cleft, which closed
as suddenly as it had opened, making a definitive pop.
Both my hands were shaking, the one holding
the knife and the one holding the bottle.
I put both objects back on the counter and breathed deeply.
"I guess this means no sangria tonight?"
said Roberta. "I'm afraid not," I said.
"I'm a very patient and easygoing man, by and large,
but I do have my limits."

December 7, 1948

In honor of the seventh anniversary of the attack on Pearl Harbor, President Truman ordered atomic bombs to be dropped on Hiroshima and Nagasaki all over again. This was the event that introduced the term "re-incineration" to modern warfare. For good measure he also commanded the Air Force to re-firebomb Tokyo. An unconfirmed rumor had it that he and Bess celebrated privately by making love that morning in the light from a radium watch dial. Very little changed in Japan, as the three cities had not yet been rebuilt following the end of World War II. In America, most citizens approved of the President's actions, and more than a few called for Dresden to be re-firebombed as well. There was a motion in the Senate for Hitler's corpse to be exhumed so that anyone willing to make the pilgrimage to Magdeburg could urinate on his charred remains. No one seconded the motion as it was generally agreed that such a move was more honor than the defeated leader of Nazi Germany deserved. Meanwhile the silent ghosts of those who had been vaporized or burned alive in Hiroshima, Nagasaki, Tokyo and Dresden looked on helplessly like all the rest of us.

Behind or Beyond

Is there anything behind or beyond?
Unknown. Insufficient data.
Most of the cerebral cortex is devoted to visual processing,
and perhaps our natural bent for pattern recognition
leads us to look for purpose and meaning
where our eyes cannot reach, in the invisible heart of things.

The year is turning, the leaves are turning, I am turning.
Into what? Questions many, answers none.
The least I can do is record my ignorance and confusion accurately.
On planet Earth I have moved a few paces north and west,
far enough to take me from those I love.
I might as well be living across the ocean

in a different century. My skills are in demand here,
and for that I receive food and drink and a third-floor window
from which to observe the coming of autumn to Red Wing, Minnesota,
a bare beauty reminding me that I am alone, I always was.
From here I can see where earth and sky appear to meet
but not whatever might be behind or beyond them both.

Twilight

The sun slowly rises
in time with my spirits, or vice versa.
Oh, I know what's really happening.
It's not a difficult concept,
the earth's rotation, though lost
for a millennium during the Dark Ages,
yet still for me and everyone else
who ever lived the sun rises, bringing hope,
that precious bit of irrationality
without which we cannot continue.
"Today may be the day!" it says, smiling.
As it happens, today is not the day.
Thank you anyway, Mr. Sun.
We needed that. Then suddenly
it's twilight, the time of sinking, of settling,
when all the ghosts rattling about
inside of us go to ground.
Where did the day go?
We can't remember, being blessed
with amnesia at just the right moment.
How fortunate for us
that this pastel purple light
is so soft and undiscriminating,
for it shines mostly
on foolishness and failure.
No matter. We're still alive,
though getting sleepier by the second,
and now is when our faithless hearts
must start worshipping the moon.

Nocturne

At this hour before morning
the colors remain indistinct,
gray that could be blue,
blue that could be purple.
There is not much difference
between dark and light,
night and day, past and present.
As the sky, so my thoughts.
Like the silent and invisible birds
I could be waiting for something to begin
if there were such a thing as time.

Morning Mist

Today we all have our heads in a cloud.
We didn't rise to meet it, it came down
To separate each of us from the crowd
And settle a silence upon the town.
Now we are even more lost in ourselves
Than usual, nothing is clear, nothing
Is sure as the beast with white fingers delves
Around and between us, seeking something
That is ancient and nameless and haunted
And apparently right under our feet.
This isn't the day we thought we wanted,
But perhaps it's the one we need, the sweet
Smell of rot in the autumn air blending
With whatever in us required mending.

Morning Likeness

Dawn creeps forward, a scout wriggling silently
toward the edge of an enemy encampment.
The yellow and orange that begin to bleed
into the pale blue are the yellow and orange of memory,
so that something utterly novel,
a new day unlike any before it,
raises tiny hairs of nostalgia on the neck.
What was comes between us and what is,
blinding us moment by moment, and yet
it's the only way we have to understand anything.
This is like *that*, though *that* is not *this*.
In such a world we are always one step behind,
the sunrise does not become real until reflected in a puddle,
the morning cries of crows surprised to find it all beginning again
cannot be heard properly until they return
as echoes from across the lake.

The New World

I was about halfway through my morning coffee when I realized
that something was different. It took me a couple of moments
to understand precisely what had changed: everything.
At some point during the night the entire universe had
been replaced by a very clever replica that was nearly
indistinguishable from the original. Only a highly aware observer
like myself would ever have noticed, which is how I concluded
that this elaborate charade was all for my benefit. I had to smile.
Don't go to such trouble on my account, Mr. Mystery Man,
or Woman, or Thing, I thought to myself. When I glanced
over at Sheryl, still snoring on the couch where she had fallen
asleep last night watching *Invasion of the Body Snatchers*,
I grasped immediately that it was not my girlfriend, not my couch,
and that last night was countless dimensions and centuries away.
In the valley outside my window, a broad, lazy-looking river
was doing an excellent impersonation of the real Mississippi,
not that I was fooled for an instant, mind you, but a person
has to make the best of things no matter what situation
they may find themselves in, and I was never one for whining.
A bird feeder that looked almost exactly like mine was being
attacked with gusto by a cardinal the color of a Hawaiian sunset.
He was practically the spitting image of the bird that used
to visit me at the crack of dawn, but why bring that up now?
It was a new world. I might as well get used to it. Every
morning is like this.

III.

The Sound of Water

Medical Report

According to the doctor I am suffering
from extreme kinetosis,
that is to say motion sickness,
usually fatal in its advanced stages
like everything else.
I wasn't surprised;
it's on both sides of the family.
I thanked him, gave him my life savings
and crawled down the steps one at a time.
Three hours later I hailed a passing wheelchair.

I've had to give up speed reading and fast women
and especially sleep,
each day I petition to stop the rotation
of the earth on its axis,
I vote to abolish elevators,
my hovercraft is up for sale.
I insist in a quiet way on my right to face the wall.

The doctor assures me I am suffering
from extreme kinetosis
or perhaps I am merely suffering.

The Sound of Water

Why this mysterious power to calm
the mind and lift the heart?
And why only in nature,
issuing from brooks, lakes and oceans?
Why not the same power
in the kitchen faucet, the bathroom shower
or the garden hose?
Is it because our ancestors
were born in water, lived and died there
never knowing the sound or smell
of the air until one of us
first clumped ashore, gasping, on bloody fins?
Driven by what? Starvation or war
or that other mystery, the will to change?
Is it that we are all exiles
longing for our true home?
Because somewhere inside each of us
the waves go on breaking
in time with our hearts?

A Treatise on Rain

I have something altogether new and original to say
about rain: it's wet, and it makes me sad.
Please stand by for further illuminations.
I feel certain the gods are speaking through me.
Heed me! Don't allow yourself to be distracted
by the rain, which is like music
in the same way that Dave Matthews is like music,
or like tears, in the same way
that my ex's tears are like tears,
which is to say, like a gangrenous old horse
pissing on a moldering fence post.
We seem to have drifted away from the subject of rain,
but have no fear, I'll get back to it
as soon as I finish mentioning four million other things
that have nothing to do with it.
Heaven forbid that any of my senseless sense impressions
should fail to be preserved for the benefit of posterity,
and posterity had damn well better appreciate
the trouble it has put me through.
O rain, rain! The splendor of your jeweled drops is—
no, scratch that. Make it snow.
Better yet, sleet. That's the ticket.

Soup Kitchen

A warm meal, a cup of coffee, a smile
and a room with a roof
and central heating is all
we have for them, the broken ones
who can never be put back together.
Each week the same faces
in the same outfits
with the same weathered hands
open, reaching their plates
forward for whatever we have to give
in place of a life with dignity.
We didn't make them.
Nothing on earth can unmake them.
Their very existence is a judgment on us.
Can there really be so many
hungry in our happy little town?
Yes. There can. There are.
Every story starts differently
but they all have the same ending,
ending here, with these empty hands
and these plates full
of what must be a poor substitute
for love.
To be part of this mournful yet
necessary exchange reveals
that we too are broken, we too are poor
and hungry.

Bach's Keyboard Concerto No. 5 in F Minor, BWV 1056 (Largo)

Here he dances with death.
The dance is quiet and slow, stately yet affectionate.
After all, they know each other well.
An orphan at ten, his own children
dropping like flies, then his beloved Maria,
and he himself shortly to be murdered
by the same quack eye doctor
who would also get away with killing the other
genius of the Baroque, Handel.
In this mesmerizing middle movement, though,
the body count falls away as we count
notes and steps in a progression
that is at once inevitable and surprising.
My heart quakes at the impossible
beauty of it, and even more at how easily
this could have been one of the many scores
lost forever after his passing,
one-third of everything he ever wrote
sold as scrap paper to wrap fish.
His own sons, not one of whom was fit
to empty his final chamber pot, thought their
father's music was overwrought, turgid, passé.
Death politely disagrees. And so
the dance continues, with Glenn Gould
and numberless others cutting in to give the cantor
of St. Thomas Church a much-needed rest,

Entropy

Scientists call it the measure of the disorder
or randomness in a system.
Too abstract?
Then reduce it to this: it's hard,
very hard, to make things better
but it's always possible to make them worse.
Thus relationships, children, companies, countries.
Entropy is the clock that forever
runs forward and down until it no longer
resembles a clock at all.
Meanwhile the love leaks out of marriages
one molecule at a time,
airlines beat passengers in their seats
and drag them screaming off the plane,
and we drop bombs on our enemies so big
they dwarf our own disorder, or so
we think, or would think, if thinking were something
still within our grasp.
I must make time in my desert of a day
to visit the grave of Robinson Jeffers and tell
his silent stone that our republic
no longer shines as it perishes
and entropy is the reason.
I'm sure that will comfort his departed shade,
long since dissipated into millions of strange shadows
by that other, more efficient entropy, death.

TSA

The furtive, too-eager groping makes me feel
like an anatomically correct abuse doll:
"Yes, mommy, that's where the bad man
touched me."
When they're finally done with their fun
they send me through the terror detector,
shoes off, belt removed, dignity and pants
both ready to fall down,
and the machine beeps me back.
"Do you have any metal in your right calf?"
Well, yes, come to think of it,
that's the one the great white shark
gnawed off at the knee.
These days it's pure aluminum
stuffed with C-4—perfectly harmless
without a detonator. Sometimes
I unscrew it and use it
to scratch my back or pound nails
or club baby seals to death.
Now Mister Happy Hands is all over me again.
"Thank you, you can go now."
No, thank *you*, officer,
thank you for keeping us all safe
from ourselves.

Life and Death and the 5th Avenue Bus

Stepping off a curb once in Manhattan
on 5th Avenue, I felt a hand
clutch my blazer near my lower spine
and yank me back on to the sidewalk
in mid-step just as a bus passed
inches in front of my face.
The sudden breeze was a delight,
especially now that I was still alive
to appreciate it. I turned
to thank my unknown benefactor
but no one's eyes met mine, nobody
seemed to want to take the credit.
That's the thing about New York,
everyone's always in such a hurry.

One Way to Die

There are psychic hemophiliacs
who bleed out from verbal paper cuts real
or imagined, it hardly matters when you
give someone that kind of power over you.

I would say to them
be a snail, move slowly if you must,
but grow your own shell
and carry it with you always.

They can't hear me though,
they're too busy preparing to swoon,
turning pale and melting in place.
To them my words are only

one more sharp edge
trying to stick a straw in their life force
the better to suck them
down to the marrow.

Ars Poetica

Remove every word
That may be inferred.

This Moment

This moment
goes by so quickly
did I see it
did I know it
as it passed
would I recognize it
if it came again
no
this moment
cannot come again
there is only one
always here
always passing
never to be grasped
never to return
the greater my desire
to hold it the more
this moment
eludes me
this moment
that is the only thing here
and that is not here
at all
this moment
calls to my emptiness
a blank mirror
recognizing a brother
this moment
a bottomless lake that is
continually drained
continually filled
it goes by so quickly
how often I forget
that everything depends
everything turns upon
this moment

Shampoo-Conditioner

(A Poem of Protest and Resistance)

How much we are fallen off from the greatness
of former times! This fallacious hybrid
pretends to do two things but does neither
well, or at all. It does not cleanse.
It cannot smooth. It clings like glue
and leaves us poorer than we started,
only now with a sodden, unkempt mess
where once was something shiny, bright
and manageable. It doesn't even rinse
honestly, this potion whose only magic
is to make everything worse. It makes me
even more ashamed to be an American,
if such a thing were possible.
When you see this compound lie, know that we
have utterly failed ourselves and our children.
It was a seemingly small task that was
asked of us, but we were not up to it,
we watchers on the wall that peer
over into a future diminished by just this much,
a little thing, yet everything that matters
is made up of a thousand little things
done with integrity and ingenuity
and pride, at the very least pride.
We settled for the easy deception,
the convenient prevarication.
Our fathers would have thrashed us senseless
before letting us descend into this abyss.
If we had any honor we would take the coins
saved by this abomination of desolation
and buy swords and fall on them.
Instead we stand in the shower blinking back
tears from the sting of a chemical
whose very name is an offense against
all that is holy. We have washed,
and yet somehow we are dirtier. And in place
of human hair we are covered in rotten straw
like the useless animals we have become.

Pumpernickel

Roberta stood at her breadboard
cutting dark, delicious slices.
Our hearts were full. Our stomachs too.
"I wonder where pumpernickel comes from?"
she said. "From the bakery," I said.
"No, silly, I mean the flour, the word,"
she said. "The word is a flower," I replied,
heedless of the dangers of homonyms.
Fifteen seconds later my smartphone had
the answer, for we live in an age of wonders.
My face darkened. "What is it?" she said,
suddenly alarmed. "Pumpernickel is a type
of rye," I said. "The word comes from the
German and refers to a side effect known as
the flatulence of Old Nick, or Satan himself."
The thought of the Lord of Hell breaking wind
should have brought us some amusement
but instead it sobered us right up.
Silently we pictured that foul, desolate blast
sweeping the earth, searching for whom
it might destroy, leveling everything in its path.
Such a wind would melt you where you stood
like a chocolate bar on the Fourth of July.
Nothing would be left but the trembling
memory of pumpernickel,
doomed, damned, demonic pumpernickel.

Fall Colors

I had already missed the beginning of the changing of the leaf guard,
and I didn't want to miss any more, so on Saturday morning
I drove to the arboretum, got out and started walking, I don't even
remember in what direction. There were a few small white clouds
in the bright blue sky, but they seemed very polite and well behaved.
I came upon a lone maple that was a stunning all-in-one exhibition of
fall colors: yellow, orange, red, brown, purple, and yes, a little green
still mixed in there. This is all the fall one man requires, I said
to myself. Or did I say it out loud? Despite the light breeze the tree
appeared to grow suddenly still, almost attentive. I smiled at my
childish fancies and picked up a single yellow leaf from the ground,
breathing in the golden honey scent. The leaf came alive in my hand,
strong, vicious, relentless. The edges were sharp as a straight razor
and it instantly took off part of my nose. Blood spurted everywhere,
and the leaf just kept coming, digging into my fingers and palm,
throwing out tiny tentacles that hissed and sucked. Too late I realized
I had encountered a rare vampire maple, and at the very hungriest
time of the year for such creatures. Dizzy with shock, I tried to shake
the leaf off, but it was no use. Dozens of other bat-like leaves
attacked my feet, ankles, calves, thighs. Blood was pouring from me now,
I was a human watering can spraying blood on everything. I gurgled
a bloody sigh and toppled over into the prettiest pile of leaves I had
ever seen. The last thing I saw was a crimson jet from my carotid artery,
and the last thing I thought was, what a lovely shade of red.

Self-Interrogation

I'm not talking.
I demand to see a lawyer,
so I leave myself in an empty
room to sweat it out
for a while. Twenty minutes of that
and I'll tell myself anything. Only
I don't.
Finally I come back smiling and
offer myself a decaf coffee
with two creams, no sugar.
Yeah, a little good cop,
bad cop. That might work.
Hey, I'm just doing my job here!
This punk is tougher
than I thought. Where were you
on the night of?
And what did she do next?
Sure, try out an alibi.
We're all ears.
We haven't heard any
funny ones lately.
Then, precisely when
I'm about to crack, I burst
through the door
with a writ of habeas corpus.

From My Mountain

Today I climbed a mountain, which was quite a feat
considering that there is no mountain,
and if there were I wouldn't have the strength to climb it.
Once I reached the top I unpacked a picnic lunch,
sat down and began to eat, sharing my meal
with the squirrels. Mountain squirrels are stronger
and hardier than their valley-born cousins,
and when they aren't begging for scraps
they like to push over pine trees and shove boulders around.
You'd best be not too slow to give them what they want.
This is all very interesting, I thought to myself,
but what about the plight of a suffering humanity?
I took the binoculars out of my backpack
and turned them on the town in the valley,
dappled with sunlight and cloud shadows.
Even with extra magnification at that height the people
were nothing but little dark dots moving slowly, like ticks.
Occasionally the dots would come together and I couldn't tell
whether they were hugging it out or one was plunging a knife
into the other. And most troubling, in the end, was there really
a difference? The uncertainty was giving me a headache.
Or rather, I realized, what was giving me a headache
was the squirrel trying to crack a nut on my skull.
Though dazed and blinded by pain, I couldn't help noticing
he was holding a rock. Quite by accident I had discovered
the first tool-using mountain squirrel!
Flushed with triumph, I started to stagger back downhill
to rejoin the rest of the little dark dots.

Cruelty

For some, it's the greatest pleasure.
In childhood, they were the ones melting ants
with a magnifying glass, pulling the wings off flies
or giving Indian burns to younger siblings.
As adults they occupy corner offices
where they enjoy summoning underlings on a rainy Friday afternoon
to ask for lengthy reports that no one will read.
Of course their genitals are shrunken almost beyond visibility
and their skulls are full of poisonous spiders locked in death embraces.
Apart from that, you might not recognize them
except for their lidless, vacant eyes, always fixed
beyond you on the pain they hope to cause you.
If you see them on the street there is no law
against running them down and backing over them again and again,
though you may get a ticket for littering.

Fall

Days grow short, like old people bending toward the earth.
Shadows, the advance guard of the night, take more territory.
Leaves let go and surrender to the great dying, the great sleep.
Wind sucks the marrow from the bones of the branches.
Painted turtles grow somnolent, sluggish, sink to the bottom of the pond,
enfold themselves in mud and begin to breathe through their skins.
The sky suddenly notices her age and applies a deeper shade of mascara,
one that complements the clouds nicely,
but like most of us she's just whistling past the graveyard.
The world, which is always trying to kill us in an offhand way,
decides to get serious about it and sends
a cold snap that bites like a dentist's drill and forms
fingers of frost that clutch at the bottoms of windows. Darkness, death
and eternity will have their say, though perhaps not the last word.

IV.

Falling in the Direction of Up

Loneliness

First off, let me say what a great subject for a poem!
I'm pretty sure no one has tackled it before,
or if they have, they were hampered by an incomplete knowledge
of the topic, whereas I, in all modesty, am an expert.
What I don't know about loneliness would fit into a thimble,
which is a lonely little place in itself
unless it's riding on a cherished finger, say,
the index finger of the last woman who truly loved me.
Here I must confess I can't recall who that was,
or when it was, or even if it ever occurred at all.
That's what happens when loneliness lives in you
like a colony of fire ants eating you from the inside out,
leaving only a set of bones too ashamed to simulate the husk of a human.
But let's not get overly dramatic, loneliness can also be
as simple as the tick of a clock that never stops,
the world's most perfect torture device if you're alone,
as I am continually, no matter who I'm with,
I might as well be serving a life sentence in solitary confinement
one cinder block wall away from the most beautiful woman on earth,
nor is it any less lonely knowing that the light from my poor
white dwarf star will not reach her for a hundred million years,
by which time it will be an exhausted, depressed light
that will not even make her blink if she chances to look up.
Forgive me, the poison of loneliness unhinges the mind
as slow and sure as rust, and can make you mix your metaphors.
Dear reader, I could tell you a lot more about loneliness
except you're not really here, I'm not certain I am either,
and I'd only be talking to myself again.

New Town

How strange to have landed in a town filled with bird shadows,
where bald eagles and turkey vultures are common as sparrows,
nestled among bluffs overlooking the Mississippi
and its endless tributaries. When these offshoots
get big enough and the water moves slowly enough,
the locals call them lakes, but a map
reveals the complicated and confusing truth.
Autumn here has no rivals, except possibly New England.
Is there anything lonelier than a beauty that cannot be shared?
When it pierces the heart like cosmic rays
there is no one and nothing to patch the holes.
For a man who continually longs for home
and who never set out to be a nomad,
I have spent my life wandering with no more purpose
than the dozens of ladybugs deceived into the foyer
of my apartment building by the promise of heat and light.
They too will perish here without meaning, unfulfilled,
but at least they will not die alone. Most of them
prepare for the end by pairing off before they stop moving,
and suddenly in the late fall sunset I am envious of insects.

The Fear

I know you're afraid
of me and what I might do to you
if you let me, just as I
am afraid of myself
alone with myself,
so quiet I can hear
the blood beating in my neck.

I fear for you also
with me or without,
in a world full
of people like us.

New Year

I resolve to forget those words
spoken or swallowed
that only varnish the tongue. Words like:
please, forever, thank-you, goodbye
and gone.
Certain phrases also must go
such as Where were you
when I called for chloroform
This must be your heart a Halloween apple
crammed with razor blades
Here cup your hands I'll pour some ashes.
I promise not to mention the mortuary
or my twin salvations
ignorance and ignominy.
I will not think of your soft feathers,
your incipient wings. I mean it,
I won't dream of your dancer's legs.
I'll stop seeing double
when there's nothing there.
I mean it.

Mementoes

During the night someone delivered
a stack of calendars,
one for each of my years left on earth.
They were novelty items,
the days numbered with zeros
already slashed out with lipstick.
The card read: "From a secret admirer."

Today it was a teacup
bearing a solitary flake of snow
from the hour of your birth.
And beside the cup a matchbook with the words:
"Make Big Money! Grow Shadows in the Privacy
of Your Own Abattoir!"

Tomorrow a fleck of dust
engraved with the story of your life
and laid like a flagstone on my lips.
The story?
"Once upon a time . . . the end."

Two Winter Haiku

Your coat has fallen
from the peg. I don't bother
to pick it back up.

* * * * *

Burning your letters—
this is the only warmth you
have ever given.

That Morning

So slow I woke I would have called it sleep,
Your breath so still I held my breath;
That morning you were mine but not to keep
While the sun, a vessel of wrath,

Poured the sullen day into our faces.
Slowly you woke. We quickly rose
And warily returned to our places.
The time goes wherever time goes.

The Heart Goes Out

The heart goes out,
The heart returns
Undone by doubt.
And then unlearns.

Two Giant Snapping Turtles Making Love

Like porcupines, they do it very carefully.
His claws are longer than hers,
no doubt so that he can cling more tightly.
Once attached, they rock and roll
gently in the swamp water,
scaring off the frogs and fish
that are their usual prey,
the waves disturbing the reeds and lily pads
that do not comprehend this form of reproduction.
Their murderous beaks and jagged green-gray shells
are hideous to look upon,
and they smell of the methane-infused mud
in which they hide and crawl every day.
Only the eight-pointed stars of their eyes
could be called beautiful,
and their unaccustomed tenderness in this moment.
Yet these wrinkled, leftover dinosaurs
give me hope that there is someone
for everyone in this world.

Overflowing

My heart is a rain barrel constantly overflowing
with love that has nowhere to go, so it goes
to the neon bar sign in the early twilight,
someplace I've never been, never will be,
yet that fuzzy red glow has won me completely,
it goes to the Cooper's hawk circling in an updraft,
yes brother, I'm with you, I too am hungry
and empty and drifting, it goes to the sound of traffic
all around me, lives hurtling by with a whoosh,
here and gone, here and gone, something whispering underneath
that speed that could be the rhythm of a slower, sadder song,
I hear you, I'm with you too, do you hear me,
it goes to the half-moon hanging like an unfinished mobile
over the crib of a star-child, it goes to the sky,
the greatest show on earth, ever-changing, ever-breathtaking,
all that beauty unfolding endlessly for everyone
but somehow so intimate also, as if unveiling itself in pink
and blue and gray just for me, yes, I'm yours, take me now!
Why do I never meet any women like that?

First Sight

Love at first sight is such a cliché
you thought
until it happened to you,
an invisible wave
passing through every particle of you
like a ghost playing a pinball machine,
instantly realigning your being,
re-magnetizing you to a new true north.
If she were an iron filing
she'd be clinging to you already.
You aren't the first
and you won't be the last.
It happened to Dante
the moment he laid eyes on Beatrice
and he immediately did the only sensible thing—
begin composing an epic poem
about the nine circles of hell.
Your fate, it seems, is kinder
and less grand—
merely to toss and turn all night
with thoughts of her,
then to rise in the morning
somehow magically refreshed.

My Dark Lovely

When we meet in the dark
my dark lovely
it's always like two subway trains
colliding and catching fire.
Many innocents are killed
but O the glory of the flames
and the sweet shudder
down the length of us
as we leap the tracks to land
atop one another.
And after, to be pulled by loving
hands from the happy wreckage
and soothed and tickled
from the edge of madness
back to sanity...
this is why I love the dark
and my dark lovely
disaster.

Love Fog

We interrupt this life with urgent news
of a love fog moving into the area.
For the next few days, visibility
will be reduced to zero
and you may not notice little things
like garbage trucks about to run you down
or air conditioners falling from second-story windows.
The fog may be accompanied
by a rapid heartbeat and a heightened sense
of why certain songs make you cry,
though right now for some reason
they will make you laugh like an imbecile.
Do not sign any financial documents
during this weather blackout, and do not remove
any article of clothing you are unwilling to lose.
Stay in bed with the covers pulled up
to your chin and ask for a pair
of soft hands to wipe your brow with a damp cloth
every few moments until the emergency passes
and the forecast calls for a prolonged yawn
and a million years of sleep.

Winter on the River

If we speak now
our breath will
cut ice. We drown.
We rub our hands
together
and they catch fire.
Smoke leaves us
when we open our mouths.

Primitive Instincts

The sudden crunch of dry leaves behind me.
In the fraction of a second
it takes to spin around
I become my ancestor,
expecting to see a saber-toothed cat
or the stone-pointed spear
of my human enemy.
Instantly I am ready to dodge,
run or kill.
But it's only you, love,
and instead the rush of adrenaline
becomes an aphrodisiac
as I clutch and kiss you
with more force than usual.
In what inner cave
does this version of me crouch,
silent, watchful?
And how many times each day
does he seek to emerge?
There is no answer
as he continues to gaze
through the campfire with my eyes.

You've Been Warned

Long as I had been searching for it,
I was taken unawares by love when it finally came for me,
like one struck in the back of the head
by a leg from a solid oaken desk. The sensation
was not unpleasant, accompanied as it was by shooting stars,
comets, bolts of lightning, small musical bluebirds
and other signs and omens from the heavens.
Naturally I had to sit for a moment to catch my breath.
When I stood again I was a new man
wearing the skin of the old one
like a master thief preparing for one last job.
I mean to steal everything you have, woman,
that I might know all that you are
and worship you properly in the dark pagan temple
of your most secret place. May I humbly suggest
you shine your spirit and gird your loins?
I intend to put you to the torch
and warm these gentle hands by the flames
for whatever time we have left in this world.

The Darkened Room

The room is made of sighs and gasps
and audible kisses, some of them on lips,
we pull the curtains not to hide from the sun
but to live these few stolen moments
in sound and touch and taste and scent,
happy to be souls wrapped in skin as sensitive
as a spider's web, happy for once to be bodies
trapped in time that rushes us up against each other
and pinned by gravity that pulls me into you
and rolls you on top of me, clinging like a limpet.
Eventually our vision reasserts its rightful dominance
and we manage to notice that the room contains
pieces of light from stars that are still exploding,
flashes of colors without names,
walls made of pure sky and wide eyes
mirrored in other eyes so close the lashes kiss.
Hush now, I want to hear your heart.
And I think I do.

Falling in the Direction of Up

*(after a catch-phrase from the 1950's British radio comedy
series the* Goon Show, *and a drawing by Michael Dunn)*

Are birds jealous of angels
because they can fly in realms beyond the physical?
Are angels jealous of birds
because they can fly without having to carry God?
Humans are jealous of both, I think,
the angels we can't see and can't even begin to prove exist
and the birds we see everyday
soaring over our heads, owning the sky in a way
we never can, despite our planes, helicopters and hot-air balloons.
We learn to covet what is near to us
yet forever beyond our reach, though it may also
be the thing that causes us to look upward
out of ourselves, beyond being into becoming.
That look took us to the moon once.
Someday it may take us to the stars.
Whatever it is we believe we are doing,
we are always either falling to earth
or falling in the direction of up.
I will fall that way if you will fall with me,
and it occurs to me now that two hands
holding each other almost make a wing.

Acknowledgements

Grateful acknowledgment is made to the following publications and their editors for first publishing most of the poems collected here:

11 Mag: "The First Time," "One Way to Die," "A Treatise on Rain"

The American Journal of Poetry: "December 7, 1948"

The Atlanta Review: "Suzie" (Winner of the *Atlanta Review* 2019 International Poetry Contest)

The Big Windows Review: "First Sight"

The Bitter Oleander: "Nocturne"

Borderlands: Texas Poetry Review: "Love Fog"

Burningword Literary Journal: "Entropy"

Clover, a Literary Rag: "Bach's Keyboard Concerto No. 5 in F Minor, BWV 1056 (Largo)" (Also a finalist in *The Furious Gazelle's* Spring 2018 Poetry Contest)

Emrys Journal: "The New Sangria"

Epos: "Night in the City"

Fjords Review: "3:07 a.m."

Former People Journal: "Medical Report," "Boodina," "Edgar Allan Crow"

The Furious Gazelle: "Flying," "The Sound of Water," "TSA," "Primitive Instincts," "Two Giant Snapping Turtles Making Love"

Grand Little Things: "Ars Poetica"

The Green Light Literary Review: "The House of Memory," "A Party"

The Harpoon Review: "Life and Death and the 5th Avenue Bus"

The Ibis Head Review: "Soup Kitchen"

The Moving Force Journal: "Twilight"

The Nervous Breakdown: "The Mystery of Evil"

The New Guard Literary Review: "Dean Natkin"

pamplemousse: "This Moment"

The Penn Review: "A Typical Weekend in My Young Life"

La Piccioletta Barca: "Morning Likeness"

Plume Poetry Journal: "Christmas Nineteen-Sixty-Something," "Notes from My Doppelganger"

Poydras Review: "The Sleep Test," "Northside Park"

Quail Bell Magazine: "Shampoo-Conditioner *(A Poem of Protest and Resistance),*" "From My Mountain," "You've Been Warned," "The Darkened Room"

Reed Magazine: "Father's Belt"

Right Hand Pointing: "The Heart Goes Out"

Rip Rap Literary Journal: "Outside it has stopped . . ."

Shot Glass Journal: "Cruelty," "Fall"

Soundings East: "Night Inventory"

South Florida Poetry Journal: "Abduction"

Star*Line: "Fall Colors"

The Stillwater Review: "Morning Mist"

The Stonecoast Review: "At the Dentist"

TAB Journal: "Burn Marks," "New Town"

Telluride Institute/Talking Gourds: "Tokyo Rose" (First Runner-up / Second Place for the Fischer Poetry Prize)

Third Coast: "Loneliness"

Third Wednesday Magazine: "The New World"

Thorn Literary Review: "Overflowing," "My Dark Lovely," "The Fear"

Triggerfish Critical Review: "Pumpernickel"

Verdad Magazine: "My Dinner with Fahey," "That Morning"

Verse-Virtual: "Mementoes," "New Year," "Self-Interrogation," "To Michael Beasley, Who Beat My Turtles to Death," "The Blizzard of 1967 (Chicago)"

Viscaria Magazine: "Two Winter Haiku"

Voices International: "Winter on the River"

Wild Roof Journal: "Behind or Beyond"

Willawaw Journal: "To the Tenth Planet"

Yemassee Journal: "Falling in the Direction of Up"

Notes

"The House of Memory" reflects on a bleak and brutalizing childhood, as seen in dreams of the house where seven feral children grew up. Only my siblings will understand all of the references, but the feel of it should be apparent to anyone.

"Father's Belt" is a persona poem—one in which a person, idea or thing speaks for itself—that I wrote following an inspiring workshop led by Marion Boyer at the 2019 Kalamazoo Poetry Festival.

"A Typical Weekend in My Young Life" records a harrowing occasion when myself and my six siblings were left in the care of a disturbed man in the midst of a cocaine and alcohol binge. How all of us are still alive and most of us are relatively sane, I'll never know.

"Dean Natkin," concerns a gentleman weed dealer who was a family friend and one of the more benign and stable influences in my young life. When I say gentleman, I mean he only sold weed to white-collar professional adults. He didn't traffic in the hard stuff or sell to children. So technically a criminal but also paradoxically one of the better human beings to cross my path. He also introduced me to the surreal comedy of my dear friends the Firesign Theatre, a primary creative influence on my own writing.

"Christmas Nineteen-Sixty-Something" may seem apocryphal or hyperbolic to anyone outside my immediate family. Perhaps this is the place to mention that we had three posters framed and hung in places of honor in our living room by our father, an advertising copywriter who admired effective propaganda, no matter the content. Those posters featured Adolf Hitler, Chairman Mao, and William F. Buckley, Jr. (from his unsuccessful 1965 campaign for Mayor of New York City).

"Tokyo Rose" tells the true and somewhat heartbreaking story of the title character, whose life intersected with that of my family slightly when she relocated to Chicago after her time in prison for treason, and opened an Asian novelties store.

"Northside Park" concerns a lovely little place known to everyone who has lived in Wheaton, Illinois. For me it was much more than a park. It was my chief refuge from a violent and unsafe home where some form of abuse was always threatening me and my siblings.

"Night in the City" was my first published poem, appearing in the now-defunct journal *Epos*, right next to a poem by Charles Bukowski. I was 16.

"My Dinner with Fahey" recounts my riotous one and only meeting with the master of what is called American Primitive Guitar Music, John Fahey, in Chicago sometime in the mid-nineties.

"December 7, 1948" could be described as *The Man in the High Castle* of prose poems, as it depicts a kind of alternative post-World War II history.

Regarding "Soup Kitchen," wherever I live I try to volunteer at a local soup kitchen, washing dishes. It's hard to write truthfully about the people served every week without sounding unintentionally cruel or condescending. In the end this is just one more experience that teaches how the world is not divided into the broken and the unbroken. It is divided into those that know they are broken and those that do not. Those that do not know are usually more dangerous, because they are constantly projecting their brokenness outward.

"Bach's Keyboard Concerto No. 5 in F Minor, BWV 1056 (Largo)" uses a favorite passage by my favorite composer to discuss the life, work and death of J.S. Bach. I first encountered Glenn Gould's recording in the film adaptation of Kurt Vonnegut's *Slaughterhouse Five*, and it has haunted me ever since. It is unfortunately true that the same quack eye doctor managed to kill both Bach and Handel.

"Entropy" takes Newton's Second Law of Thermodynamics and applies it—unscientifically but I think justifiably—to human affairs. The end of the poem refers to one of the most famous poems by Robinson Jeffers, called "Shine, Perishing Republic," a great poem of genuine protest that is still relevant today. The next-to-last line quotes without attribution from Shakespeare's Sonnet 53, where the meaning of the evocative phrase "millions of strange shadows" is not entirely clear. I take it as a metaphor for the mysterious complexity of the human mind and spirit, a complexity reduced to mere chaos by entropy. Except that to go from one "departed shade" to "millions of strange shadows" could also imply a reversal of entropy, an increase in ordered complexity and humanness, a scientific impossibility but perhaps a spiritual possibility.

"From My Mountain" is an attempt to be funny and serious at the same time. I also thought it would be interesting to dive right in with an unreliable narrator and then proceed as if nothing had happened.

"Two Winter Haiku" tries to follow some of the countless rules for writing haiku. One of the oldest and most traditional is that they should be nature-based, or at least contain some seasonal element. These are about a breakup that occurred in winter, and both refer to the season, at least by implication.

"Primitive Instincts" was inspired by recent readings in evolutionary psychology.

"Falling in the Direction of Up" has a winding history. I had already decided that I wanted it to be the title of this, my first full-length poetry collection. The title is adapted from a catch-phrase from the 1950's British radio comedy series the *Goon Show*, where the young Peter Sellers got his start. When the Beatles met their producer George Martin, they didn't care what other musical acts he had worked with, but they were terribly impressed that he had made records with the Goons. That's how they knew they'd get on with him. One of the characters in the show would sometimes refer to "falling in the direction of down," a funny phrase that I simply turned around to sound slightly uplifting, perhaps influenced by Maya Angelou's "Still I Rise." However, I didn't have a title poem to go with the title! Then some people organized an art exhibit of fascinating drawings by Michael Dunn at the People's Church in Kalamazoo and asked if I could contribute something (each drawing was accompanied by an ekphrastic poem). One drawing featured a bird, an angel and a woman's face, and the poem came together very quickly after that.

Photo credit: Scott Erskine

Kurt Luchs was born in Cheektowaga, New York, grew up in Wheaton, Illinois, and has lived and worked all over the United States. He could give his current location, but it would probably have changed by the time you read this, and it would only make it easier for the bounty hunters to find him. Like the founders of Rome, he was raised by wolves (see the first section of this book). Like Grandma Moses, he had no formal training and began his artistic pursuits late in life, though in all honesty it must be said that his embroidery work is nothing to write home about. After years of writing humor for the *New Yorker*, the *Onion* and *McSweeney's Internet Tendency*, among others, he returned to his first love, poetry, like a wounded animal crawling into its burrow to die. In 2017 Sagging Meniscus Press published his humor collection, *It's Funny Until Someone Loses an Eye (Then It's Really Funny)*, which has since become an international non-bestseller. In 2019 his poetry chapbook *One of These Things Is Not Like the Other* was published by Finishing Line Press, and he won the *Atlanta Review* International Poetry Contest, proving that dreams can still come true and clerical errors can still happen.

www.ingramcontent.com/pod-product-compliance
Lightning Source LLC
Chambersburg PA
CBHW020211090426
42734CB00008B/1023